WORLDLY HOLINESS

WORLDLY HOLINESS

R. Benjamin Garrison

ABINGDON PRESS
nashville . new york

2/84PGC

WORLDLY HOLINESS

ISBN 0-687-46336-X

Library of Congress Catalog Card Number: 72-172808

MANUFACTURED BY THE PARTHENON PRESS AT
NASHVILLE, TENNESSEE, UNITED STATES OF AMERICA

For My Parents
Eilene Kendall
and
Claude Garrison
My first and best tutors

PREFACE

The popular modern, and perhaps stereotypical, view of Francis of Assisi is sketched by a twentieth-century poet who contrasts himself with this strangely compelling figure from the thirteenth century. The poet laments:

I never whittle away time purging my mind
as St. Francis of Assisi who made faces at his body
while tying the libido with the rough rope of discipline . . .[1]

However, Francis was an ascetic only in the sense that any good soldier is—disciplined, trained, ready, tested, unencumbered.

The word "worldly" has shifted meaning, meaningfully, in recent theological literature. Superficially Francis' concept of "world" might seem to harmonize with

---

[1] William Walter DeBolt, "A Modern Pharisee Talks to Himself," copyright 1970, Christian Century Foundation. Reprinted by permission from *The Christian Century*, May 20, 1970.

the older signification of the word, judging from his peculiar attire, his rejection of things (or of some things anyway), his poverty. Yet on another hand he was very worldly, in an astringently modern sense. He embraced the world, as anyone knows who has ever attentively hymned the Saint's canticle to the sun and the moon. He felt responsible for every creature that came within his ken or crossed his path.

His classic prayer is thus, on our terms, refreshingly worldly, as the reflections that make up this book will attempt to show. The ancient virtues that his prayer enjoins and enables—peace, love, pardon, faith, joy, understanding, benevolence—are as contemporary as this evening's newscast but a good deal more enduring. The reason that this prayer of St. Francis is permanently newsworthy is that it is rooted, in turn, in the New Testament's Good News.

What follows is an attempt to take seriously the modern Christian's necessarily ambiguous relationship to the world as something to be both resisted and embraced. This book is also an effort to help the Christian of today understand and appropriate those virtues and graces, those strengths and gifts, which are re-presented in the prayer. Throughout I have tried to hold the classic prayer and the modern world in radically serious tension without permitting either to dissolve into the other.

As with my earlier books, I am grateful for the helpfully critical, if sometimes antiseptic, comments of several people: my father, Claude Garrison; my former professors, Alfred Burton Haas and Edna Hayes Taylor; my former student, Iris Knell; and Ruth Stillwell of the department of English at the University of Illinois.

I am joyfully obliged to name another person, whose critique has been pivotal, and she is Vibeke Schousboe. Few exercises in understanding are more revealing than that of viewing the gospel through the eyes of someone who is seeing it for the first time.[2] That observation is especially germane here, in a double sense: Vibeke became a Christian in adulthood; English is not her native tongue. From that twin and fresh perspective she has argued with my ideas, questioned my vocabulary, and clarified my thought. She would not expect me to accept all her suggestions, and I have not done so. Nevertheless, both the book and I have been improved because of her gentle bludgeon.

Even with the substantial assistance of all these people, however, this manuscript would not have "happened" without the generous annual study leave which my congregation, the Wesley United Methodist Church of Urbana-Champaign, Illinois, has accorded me for more than a decade. I wish also to thank Louise Gish, who has made the customary term "faithful secretary" both a redundancy and an understatement. Also Mr. and Mrs. Raymond Vogel affectionately nit-picked the page proofs. Additionally, my wife has affirmed the "for better, for worse" part of our vows by thoughtfully

[2] See chapter on "Joy," p. 62.

examining most of the earlier drafts. Her help has been especially fruitful.

Finally, I am thankful for the long-term influence of my parents, not so much directly upon the book but very decisively upon the author. I have dedicated the volume to them because they are vital enfleshments of the sort of worldliness and the kind of holiness I have tried to write about herein.

R. Benjamin Garrison

CONTENTS

Lord,
make us instruments of thy peace.
Where there is hatred, let us sow love;
where there is injury, pardon;
where there is discord, union;
where there is doubt, faith;
where there is despair, hope;
where there is darkness, light;
where there is sadness, joy.
O divine Master,
grant that we may not so much seek
to be consoled as to console;
to be understood as to understand;
to be loved as to love;
for it is in giving that we receive;
it is in pardoning that we are pardoned;
and it is in dying that we are born
to eternal life.

—Francis of Assisi

1
The Seed of Peace

"Lord, make us instruments of thy peace."

History has combined his nickname and his hometown and called him a saint. Almost nobody knows who Giovanni Bernardone was. But nearly everybody has heard of Francis of Assisi. Francesco (the little Frenchman), so called because of his love for the wandering Gaelic troubadours; Assisi, the Italian place of his birth and death.

He strikes me as a strange combination of the antiquated and the up-to-date. As we see him under yonder tree, first talking to the birds and then turning his face upward to sing a good morning greeting to the rising sun (which he calls his brother), our first reaction is to suppose that the poor chap has taken leave of his senses. That at least is what many of his contemporaries concluded. After all, the son of a wealthy cloth merchant does not usually renounce his legacy, resign his military commission, and go about in rags. Perhaps he was the original flower child.

One of his flowers is a prayer. That is where the up-to-date part comes in. It is printed at the beginning of this book. Its meaning and aspirations will occupy us in this book under the rubric, "Worldly Holiness." In this chapter we will reflect upon its opening phrase, "O Lord, make us instruments of thy peace."

The outline leaps out at us: (1) We have a Lord. (2) We are to be his instruments (3) for the provision of a particular kind of peace, his kind.

"Lord . . ."

From the beginning Christians have differed sharply and sometimes not too politely about how best to interpret the significance of Jesus. Even in the New Testament the range was wide, the statements were varied. Matthew and Luke, wanting to emphasize the utter humanity of the man, said he was born of a woman. That stood in intentional contrast to other ancient religions whose deities, the Greeks said, sprang from the head of Jupiter, out of the nowhere into the here. John, wanting to stress the eternal significance of Jesus, spoke of him as the word God uttered into history, "the Word made flesh." There is a fascinating phrase in Galatians (2:11) in which Paul said that he "withstood" brother Peter to his "face." That is nothing but a pious cover-up by whoever took the minutes of that meeting. Roughly translated it means, "We had one beaut of a fight." And so across the centuries—Jesus has had almost as many interpretations as he has had interpreters.

Usually, however, Christians have not disagreed about his right to the title "Lord." To be sure, the word has for us an unfortunately medieval cast, conjuring up images of castles and serfs and subservience. But it need not be so.

Its older meaning, its finer signification, is finely caught in John Wesley's covenant prayer, "I am no longer my own, but thine." To call Jesus "Lord" is to make a statement about ownership and obligation, not about privilege and power. It is essentially a pledge of allegiance.

I get the feeling that the word "Lord" referring to Jesus has a limited viability in the twentieth century. But the fact which the word is intended to convey is as contemporary as our latest failure or our next aspiration. Messiah, Christ, and Lord are approximately equivalent terms: Messiah, the Coming One; Christ, the Anointed One; Lord, the Reigning or Ruling One. His words sang and his deeds rang with authority. He even died with authority. Nobody took his life from him. Rather, as John affirms, he freely "laid down his life for us" (I John 3:16). It is that authority which the word "Lord" is intended to acknowledge and underline.

This lordly fact, commanding and demanding, used to bother me as a young man. I did not want an owner, a lord. I wanted to be my own boss. Then one day I looked deep into my heart and discovered that I was not and could not be my own boss. I was bound to bind myself to something, to liege myself to some lord. It might be money or success, education or reason, pleasure or self—anyway, something. The question was not whether I would have a lord but what or who it would be. So as a youth I was guided to see that one might as well have a lord who measured up to the job description. Like lots of persons before me, I discovered that it took lots of lord to master me. But I also discovered that this Jesus could do and did. And so a Christian began to be born.

Anyway, this is where Francis began, with one he could no longer escape or safely ignore. He resigned from the army, but he did not delude himself into supposing that he was no longer commissioned or commanded. He had been called "a new sort of Christian soldier." [1] He had found his commander, his sovereign, his Lord.

"make us instruments"

This is where the image of instruments applies. "Lord, make us instruments . . ." We might better understand the pointedness of this prayer if we prayed it rather, "O Lord, make us *implements.* Finely forge us into scalpels of the spirit, sharpened to cut out what-

[1] Henry and Dana Thomas, *Living Biographies of Religious Leaders* (Garden City, N. Y.: Blue Ribbon Books, 1946), p. 131.

ever obstructs life and health and peace. Hammer us into deep-digging plows that lay back the soil of men's lives so that they can be seeded and fruitful. Lay hold upon the rude handles of our lives and use us in fashioning thy peaceable kingdom. Lord, make us instruments."

Who, me? The protest may be honest and understandable, but not, for the Christian, permissible. "No Christian should ever think or say that he is not fit to be God's instrument, for that in fact is what it means to be a Christian. We may be humble about many things, but we may never decline to be used." [2] True, we are not yet fit instruments or ever perfect ones.

> All of us alike are God's instruments. By no setting of our hearts on wickedness or doing evil with both our hands can we prevent God from using us. Our folly will serve Him, when our wisdom fails; our wrath praise Him, though our wills rebel. Yet, as God's instruments without intention and in our own despite, we generally serve God's ends only as we defeat our own.[3]

We have to be *made* into his instruments. But that is another matter, his matter. Ours is but to pray, in the words of an old hymn, "Have thine own way, Lord . . . Mold me and make me . . ."

Notice, by the way, that the Franciscan prayer is not,

---

[2] Alan Paton, *Instrument of Thy Peace* (New York: Seabury Press, 1968), pp. 15-16.

[3] John Oman, *The Paradox of the World* (Cambridge: Cambridge University Press, 1921), p. 30.

"Lord, make us *recipients* of thy peace." For "the moment peace is sought as life's most desirable goal, it is lost." [4] That, I judge, is about equally true of international peace and of inner peace. The peace we seek is for the road, not for the lounge; for life's laboratories, not for its resting places. It is worth noting and pondering that, when Jesus promised his own peace to his disciples, it was the night before he died. It is a peace for expenditure, for exertion, for use, not for saving up or saving back. It is a peace for investment, not for hoarding.

It happens sometimes that we *are* the recipients of Christ's peace, as he himself promised in that last codicil to his will, according to the terms of which he bequeathed to us the peace that the world cannot give. But if our eyes are upon the main peaceful chance for ourselves, it is likely that we will not have the eyes to see it or the heart to receive it, even if it is right before our eyes. "Lord, make us instruments, implements, utensils of thy peace."

"of thy peace"

It is important to note that an inherent ambiguity nides at the heart of the word "peace" as we have been using it here. It can refer either to an inner state or to

---

[4] John Mackay, *God's Order* (New York: Macmillan, 1953), p. 114.

an outer condition or to both. Peace is personal. Peace is also social. The two are connected.

It is also helpful to note what is *not* intended or implied by the word. The Oxford Dictionary gives the following as a subordinate definition of peace: "absence of noise, movement, or activity." I am very much afraid that we too often, though unconsciously, make that a primary meaning for peace. "Why can't we have a little peace around here!" That is: shut up, slow down, stay home. This spurious peace was perfectly paraphrased by that great American "philosopher," Al Capone. He said, "We don't want no trouble."

Now, quite honestly, is it not true that we mistake that for peace? If our personal lives are quiet and uncomplicated, unstretched or undemanding, we call that hollowness "peace." If no marchers mar our streets and no protesters disturb our calm, if law is not openly flouted and order not actually attacked—that is, if in Capone's terms "we don't have no trouble"—we dub the deception "peace." It is probably closer to caution or exhaustion or emptiness or unconcern. But we call it peace.

What, then, are the special qualities of genuine, positive peace? Reinhold Niebuhr suggests that the peace of God surpasses understanding precisely because it "contains the pains and sorrows of suffering love."[5] It claims no exemption from disappointment, failure,

[5] *The Self and the Dramas of History* (New York: Scribner's, 1955), p. 226.

trouble, and fear. The peace that passes understanding is a way of embracing, not of escaping, the vicissitudes that otherwise would sap our vitality, attack our stability, and immobilize us in midstream. It enables us to heed the prophet's admonition, "Do not call conspiracy all that this people call conspiracy, and do not fear what they fear, nor be in dread " (Isaiah 8:12).

The makeup of this godly peace, of which we are to be both exemplars and instruments, is interestingly pointed toward in

> three Chinese characters, all similarly translated "peace." The first, *ping,* suggests equality. Peace obtains where no one seeks to domineer over another. The second, *an,* is an ideograph representing a woman under a roof. Peace obtains when homes are unmolested and tranquil. The third, *ho,* is a character combining two elements, mouth and grain. Peace obtains when all have sufficient to eat.[6]

Equity, security, prosperity. It is, I suppose, possible to possess a measure of peace without all three. But it is not likely.

One could without difficulty provide a potpourri of scripture in which the words "peace" and "pursue" recur in tandem. Samples: "seek peace, and pursue it" (Psalms 34:14). "Let us then pursue what makes for peace" (Romans 14:19). "Let him seek peace and pursue it" (I Peter 3:11*b*). This pursuit factor, better than

---

[6] T. Z. Koo as related in *Interpreter's Bible* (Nashville: Abingdon Press, 1957), XII, 52a.

anything else, emphasizes the biblical conviction that peace is not a passive quality. It is something we go in pursuit after, not frantically and hopelessly but confidently and relentlessly. "Blessed are the peace*makers*" said Jesus. To *make* peace is to conceive, construct, and consecrate those conditions which enable it. It is to work under the profound conviction that we labor not alone. "Did we in our own strength confide, our striving would be losing" (Luther). Because of such cosmic comradeship Christians are able to be sublimely reckless in their pursuit of peace. Since they have it within, they can, and must, build it without.

This chapter is entitled the *seed* of peace. The imagery is instructive. Botanists tell us that seeds are important means of carrying plant life over periods unfavorable for growth and of distributing the plant in space and time. Some seeds germinate only after exposure to the light. Furthermore, some legume seeds, known to be more than a hundred years old, have germinated. The oriental lotus has flowered after lying dormant a thousand years.

The imagery, I say, is instructive. It is starkly clear that ours is a time grossly unfavorable to the growth of the plant of peace. But its seeds must be preserved, nourished, moistened by the waters of sacrifice and exposed to the light of reason. Peace is a tardy legume or an ancient lotus. But it can flower.

And will—if we will. A Vietnam veteran said to me recently, "What we are doing there is an obscenity—a gross obscenity." The increasing ability to see that and the increasing willingness to say that constitute germinating light, however glimmering. The reader may have occasion to be in Washington, D.C., from time to time. If you pass by the White House you will notice a small band of citizens who are frequently watching and fasting, hard by the seat of power and the center of decision. They are moistening the seed. You might consider standing with them for a day or an hour. Others may wish to join in the Sunday services held in various churches, services designed to keep the soil raked and ready for the plant of peace to push its tender bloom into our midst. Still others will fertilize this fragile flower with their checkbooks. Thus we ready the seedling planted in the providence of God by the Prince of Peace.

Many of you will recall that passage of inspired beauty and italicized truth with which Norman Cousins concludes his book, *In Place of Folly*. The essay is entitled "Checklist of Enemies" (the reference is to enemies of peace). In it this modern prophet with a pen writes:

> The enemy is many people. He is a man whose only concern about the world is that it stay in one piece during his own lifetime. . . .
>
> The enemy is a man who has a total willingness to delegate his worries about the world to officialdom. He assumes that only the people in authority are in a position to know and act. . . . If a problem is wholly or partially scientific in nature, he will ask no questions even though

> the consequences of the problem are political or social. . . .
>
> The enemy is any man in government, high or low, who keeps waiting for a public mandate before he can develop big ideas of his own, but who does little or nothing to bring about such a mandate. Along with this goes an obsessive fear of criticism. To such a man, the worst thing in the world that can happen is to be accused of not being tough-minded in the nation's dealings with other governments. He can take in his stride, however, the accusation that he is doing something that may result in grave injury to the human race. . . .
>
> The enemy is any man in the pulpit who . . . talks about the sacredness of life but . . . never relates that concept to the real and specific threats that exist today to such sacredness. He identifies himself as a man of God but feels no urge to speak out against a situation in which the nature of man is likely to be altered and cheapened, the genetic integrity of man punctured, and distant generations condemned to a lower species. He is a dispenser of balm rather than an awakener of conscience. He is preoccupied with the need to provide personal peace of mind rather than to create a blazing sense of restlessness to set things right. He is an enemy because the crisis today is as much a spiritual crisis as it is a political one.[7]

The instrument of peace also is many people. He too is concerned that the world "stay in one piece during his own lifetime." But he has, or wants, children or grandchildren and so is concerned about those practical decisions which affect his offspring and theirs.

The instrument of peace is stalwartly unwilling to

[7] (New York: Harper, 1961), pp. 206-8.

assign his worries to Washington. Precisely *because* the issues are so grave and the outcome is so portentous, he demands that his government level with him. He listens to the experts, but he also expects them to listen to him.

The instrument of peace is the government official who ponders, plans, and leads without being dominated by the weight of his mail or the size of his opposition. He is tough-minded, but he is also open-minded.

The instrument of peace is the pastor or rabbi who knows that few things become real until they become local. He aims to comfort the afflicted, but he also aims to afflict the comfortable.

The instrument of peace is the man or woman in the pew who is willing to be used or laid aside, recognized or ignored, working through his prayers and praying through his work that God's will be done, his kingdom come, on earth.

Lord, make us instruments of *thy* peace.

2
The Seed of Selfhood

"Where there is hatred, let us sow love. . . .
Grant that we may not so much
Seek . . . to be loved as to love."

> Man is . . . the little creature who is forever seeking himself, and therefore also fleeing from himself; one who is forever being drawn and attracted by something higher, and yet is ever seeking to release himself from this higher element; the creature who is both aware of his contradiction and yet at the same time denies it.[1]

In these provocative and paradoxical terms one of this century's major theologians describes man: you, me.

---

[1] Emil Brunner, *Man in Revolt* (Philadelphia: Westminster Press, 1947), pp. 24-25.

Focus your attention for a moment upon that opening clause: "Man is . . . the little creature who is forever seeking himself, and therefore also fleeing from himself." Man's search for selfhood is as old as he is. It is his most primitive pilgrimage as well as his most recent one. It continues uncompleted.

Here is our prehistoric ancestor standing at the opening of his cave, his brow furrowed at wonderment about who he is and how he differs from his distant cousins swinging in the trees. Here is the psalmist crying out, "O Lord . . . I am languishing" (6:2a) or expressing *his* wonderment, "What is man that thou art mindful of him?" (8:4a). Here is a full-grown man asking Jesus what he must do to be born. Here is Ibsen's Peer Gynt. He sought to be the Emperor of Self. He was always ready to talk of his soul, as the Troll King reminded him, but actually he heeded nothing except the tangible. Here is a person, young or not so young, just back from a bad trip on LSD. Here are people in their seldom-completed search for selfhood.

Francis, whose prayer is engaging our attention throughout this book, has to be counted among the more successful of this uneven company of searchers. A couple of the phrases of this prayer may constitute a clue as to why:

> Where there is hatred, let us sow love . . .
> Grant that we may not so much
> Seek . . . to be loved as to love . . .

THE SEED OF SELFHOOD

I

If the self has proved hard to find, it has been equally difficult to define, even by the intellectually sophisticated. Socrates in his famous aphorism enjoined each of us to "know thyself." He did not, however, clarify what this self was that we are supposed to know. The prodigal in Jesus' even more famous parable "came to him*self*." Presumably this implied an uncomfortable clarity about who he was and how he got that way, but, once more, we are not told just what he saw in the mirror of his failure. We can find few grounds for faulting Shakespeare's advice, "To thine own self be true," but still the question remains, Which self is really mine? Modern literature, too, is crowded to the dust jackets with characters who are forever clasping a stethoscope to their own chests in an endless effort to hear what makes them tick, what self beats beneath their anxieties or pumps blood into their hopes. One thinks of Willy Loman in *Death of a Salesman*, of Julia in *The Cocktail Party*, of Holden Caulfield in *Catcher in the Rye*, to name but some of thousands. The human self is omnipresent but elusive.

For the moment let us simply go with the following attempt at definition: the human self is that complex of hopefully harmonious characteristics which makes a person what he essentially is. As such it changes—I change—from day to day, from experience to experience. It includes my dominant desires and my overreaching purposes. It is shaped by both my failures and my faith. It includes all that I once was and, potentially, all that I seek to be. "The self does not leave its past behind as the moving hand of a clock does; its past is inscribed into it more deeply than the past of geologic formations is crystallized in their present form." [2] That description of the self is, I admit, vague enough, but that is not my fault. It is precisely the shifting boundaries of the self which constitute our continual problem. The self we get to know today is altered by the morrow. It is still present but not still the same.

One more thing, a warning, before we move to a more direct consideration of love as the seed of selfhood. Christians have sometimes indulged in a deal of loose talk about the self, pronouncing it as if it were a kind of theological cuss word. The insinuation has been that the self is an evil entity, one that proper people might unfortunately possess but must never admit. Paul Tillich has consequently warned us that "it is time to end the bad theological usage of jumping with moral indignation on every word in which the syllable 'self' appears." [3] We sometimes carelessly speak of a "self-*less* person," a phrase as nonsensical as "mindless genius" or "legless highjumper." A man may have a good self or an evil one, a twisted self or a whole one. But he cannot in any literal sense be self*less*.

---

[2] H. R. Niebuhr, *The Responsible Self* (New York: Harper, 1963), p. 93.

[3] *The Courage to Be* (New Haven: Yale University Press, 1952), p. 87.

II

While I was pondering a way to get a hold on the basic idea of this chapter, I happened upon some philosophy notes taken down by my clergyman-grandfather seventy years ago while he was an undergraduate at DePauw University. Once more old Gramp came to my rescue. The lecture dealt with the philosopher and scientist, René Descartes, the father of modern rationalism. Philosophy students will recall how the great Frenchman set out methodically to doubt everything. Finally he arrived at a formula that came out something like this: "I doubt, says he: that is absolutely certain. Now, to doubt is to think. Hence it is certain that I think. To think is to exist. Hence it is certain that I exist. *Cogito, ergo sum.*" [4] I think, therefore I am.

One of my teachers at Cambridge altered this famous Cartesian formula in a most suggestive and helpful way. "I would be prepared," he declared, "to argue for the proposition, 'I am loved, therefore I am' " (Peter Baelz). What makes me *me,* what flings me into existence, is the fact that I am loved. This forms me, fills me, makes me. The seed of my selfhood is the fact that I have been loved into life.

The evidence for this is everywhere. From the ghetto to the suburbs we see children who are emotionally retarded because love has not taught them life's letters.

---

[4] Alfred Weber, *History of Philosophy* (New York: Scribner's, 1902), pp. 308-9.

The divorce courts listen to pathetic creatures who are physically adult but spiritually infantile, stunted selves who cannot give love because they have not received it. On the other hand, golden wedding anniversaries are often—not always,[5] but often—glad testimonies to the positive side of this truth. We need to be careful about speaking of love as if it could be quantified like gasoline or mutual funds. But the capacity to love can be *qualified,* lastingly fulfilled or permanently crippled by the way in which love is offered or withheld.

One popular and pernicious concept of love sees it as the emotional counterpart of the marshmallow—a soft substance made up mostly of sugar-water and gelatin. Love is always kind, as Paul contended, but it is not always pliant, pleasant, or even predictable.

Read the book *Take One Step,*[6] about a child afflicted with cerebral palsy and about her parents' efforts to force her to take that step. A dollar bill is pinned to the window curtains. "When you walk to the window and retrieve the dollar, we'll go out and buy some doll clothes with it." The child steps, stumbles, falls, pulls the curtains down with her. The mother rehangs the curtains, repins the money, and repeats the command. Then one day the child walked. She was literally loved into health, not very gently but very firmly. Sometimes

---

[5] Sometimes they are what Samuel Johnson called the triumph of hope over experience.

[6] Evelyn W. Ayrault (New York: Modern Library, 1963).

there is more love in a strike or a blow than in a stroke or a kiss.

Anyway, the New Testament understood long before George Herbert Mead did that a person becomes a person only in a society of other persons, that love is elicited by a prior love. "We love," cries John, "because he first loved us" (I John 4:19). "I find, I walk, I love," sings the hymnwriter, "but oh, the whole of love is but my answer, Lord, to thee!" 'Tis a truth not limitable to the divine. We love in every case because someone first placed his life beneath our own and loved us out of ourselves. We find and love because we have been found and loved. The whole of love is but an answer.

This is the reason Paul could say in Colossians:

> as the Lord has forgiven you, so you also must forgive. And above all these put on love, which binds everything together in perfect harmony. And let the peace of Christ rule in your hearts. . . . (3:13*b*-15a)

Now consider that same passage once more, only this time in a modern translation titled vividly *The Cotton Patch Version of Paul's Epistles:*

> Put up with one another, and freely forgive each other if one has a gripe against somebody. You all forgive as freely as the Lord forgave you. Over all these things wear love, which is the robe of maturity. And let Christ's peace . . . order your lives.[7]

---

[7] Clarence Jordan (New York: Association Press, 1968).

Liken it to this: amateur photographers sometimes accidentally take two pictures on one spot of film, thus getting a "double exposure," two pictures on the same print, one superimposed on the other. Something like this happens to the life exposed to the love of God. What is unlovely is not thereby removed from the film. But over it are now seen the outlines of another picture which give texture and meaning to the dark photograph of failure beneath. Where there was hatred, now there is love. Where there was injury, pardon; where there was doubt, faith; where there was despair, hope; where there was darkness, light; and where there was sadness, joy. The picture of man's life is lightened and enlivened by the love of God.

The idea that personhood becomes full only as it responds has, I think, an important implication for our understanding of God. However much violence it may do to our traditional doctrines, does this not mean that God changes—dare we say that God becomes more godly—as we respond to him in love? The Bible tells us that ours is a living God. Living involves and requires changing. The God and Father of our Lord Jesus Christ is great enough to grow, to shape new stratagems of compassion, to take new risks of sacrifice, to assume new forms of love—in short to respond to our responses.

III

Let me see whether I can pull all this together by way of one of the deathless dramas out of Scandinavia, namely, Ibsen's *Peer Gynt*. Peer, you will recall, was passionately bent upon being himself, but, like lots of us, he did not rightly know what or who that self was that he was trying to be. Nevertheless, he set out with a vengeance.

He left Solveig, his beloved, to become a man of the world. He was commercially successful as a slave merchant (although he fed and educated his chattels). He was romantically successful as a lover. Still the emptiness he tried to leave behind in Norway left Norway with him. One time in the mountains he heard a voice and, startled, asked, "Who are you?" "Myself," the voice replied, and then added accusingly, "Can you say as much?" [8] Once, on a return trip home, he says to his mother: "Let's put off serious thinking till later . . . let's have a gossip and talk of all sorts of things, except what's ugly and horrid and hurts—let's forget all that" (p. 1,098). In middle age in far-off Morocco he says to a German gentleman: "What's a man's first duty? . . . To be himself—to take good care of all that touches himself and what is his. But how can he do this if his existence is that of a pack-camel laden with someone else's weal and woe?" (p. 1,103).

He was, in that moment, quite close to the truth, without ever recognizing it. Another time, he accuses some acquaintances in an insane asylum of being outside themselves. Begriffenfeldt replies, "Oh, no. It's

---

[8] *Eleven Plays of Henrik Ibsen* (New York: Modern Library), p. 1,083. Page references throughout are to this edition.

here that men are most themselves—themselves and nothing but themselves—sailing with outspread sails of self. Each shuts himself in a cask of self, the cask stopped with a bung of self and seasoned in a well of self. None has a tear for others' woes or cares what any other thinks. We are ourselves in thought and voice—ourselves up to the very limit" (p. 1,138).

Still another time, on a misty moor at night, he hears some haunting, taunting voices singing:

> We are thoughts;
> You should have thought us . . .
> We are tears
> Which were never shed . . .
> We are deeds
> You have left undone . . .

"Rubbish!" cries Gynt. "You can't condemn a man for actions that he *hasn't* done!" (Pp. 1,163-65.)

Finally, late in life, the Button Moulder tells him, "You never yet have been yourself" (p. 1,169). Gynt finally believes it. Heartsick, self-condemned, defeated, but honest at last, he makes his way back to Norway and to the aging Solveig. In soul-shaking despair he cries out to her, speaking of his elusive self, "Can you tell me where Peer Gynt has been since last we met? . . . With the mark of destiny on his brow—the man that he was when a thought of God's created him! "Can you tell me that? . . . Where was my real self . . . the Peer Gynt who bore the stamp of God upon his brow?" And

Solveig replies, smiling softly: "In my faith, in my hope, and in my love" (p. 1,184).

That's where we all are, if we are at all—in another's faith and hope and love.

One of the early critics of this manuscript delivered a deserved, though affectionate, theological rebuke. Noting that I had written the prayer of St. Francis in the plural instead of the singular, as it is often seen—"Lord, make us" instead of "Lord, make me"—he said, "I understand why you did that. I understand the need for community. But I wonder whether you're not letting *me* off too easily. I'm perfectly willing to let *them* be instruments of God, or even for *us* to be instruments of God. But I'm not sure I myself am willing."

The reminder was apt. It cannot happen in them or in us until it happens in you and in me. The Christian holiness the world so needs and deserves can only occur one person at a time. Persons are born only as they are loved. "Ultimately there is only one place of refuge on this planet for any man—that is in another man's heart. To love is to make of one's heart a swinging door." [9]

Then, when you have made your heart a door that swings in both directions, you are able at last maturely to pray, "Grant that we may not so much seek to be loved as to love."

---

[9] Howard Thurman, *Disciplines of the Spirit* (New York: Harper, 1963), p. 127.

3
The Seed of Forgiveness

"where there is injury, pardon. . . .
It is in pardoning that we are pardoned."

It is hard to know who is the more pathetic, the unforgiving man or the unforgiven man. The one doubts the necessity of forgiveness, the other doubts the possibility of forgiveness. Both are about equidistant from the gospel, and it is not a short distance.

The older I grow the angrier I become with those twisted versions of the gospel which leave people emotionally stunted, psychologically crippled, and spiritually sterile. Such distortions turn normal, growing people into perfectionists who cannot accept themselves or anyone else as they are. The god they mistakenly worship is a bloated version of an angry old man more appropriately scorned than honored. The end result is that the human creature, who should be plastic, growing, and beautiful, is hardened, immobilized, and embittered; unforgiving, unforgiven, and unfulfilled.

It is precisely here that the insight of St. Francis is so penetrating. The phrase of his prayer which invites our attention in this chapter is the petition, "Where there is injury (let us sow) pardon . . . for . . . it is in pardoning that we are pardoned. . . ."

I

The ground of forgiveness is need.

I would not want what I wrote above to be taken to mean that only legalistic religion produces unforgiving people. Nor do I imply a casualness about the human condition which sits lightly to our failures, foibles, follies, and faithlessness. Quite the opposite, the need for forgiveness—for release, for healing, for wholeness—is universal. It is perhaps the one thing we all have in common. It is our basic democracy. "All we like sheep have gone astray . . ." (Isaiah 53:6).

This is perhaps most evident among those who deny it. One of the refreshing, if occasionally unnerving, things about the Bible is its antiseptic honesty in the face of pesky human stupidity, cupidity, and deception. Consider, for instance, this hunk of self-deception which somehow sneaked its way into the literature of piety. It is found in Psalm 18:20-24:

> The Lord rewarded me according to my righteousness; . . .
> For I have kept the ways of the Lord,
> and have not wickedly departed from my God.
> For all his ordinances . . . and his statutes I did not put away from me.
> I was blameless before him,
> and I kept myself from guilt.
> Therefore the Lord has recompensed me according to my righteousness.

How nice! Such a person would not be able to recognize forgiveness if you rubbed his soul in it.

I suppose it is this perennial propensity to cheat on our spiritual tax returns which makes it so difficult for some of us to say those two little words, "I'm sorry." They can of course be said too easily, in flippant disregard for the fact that they should mean, "I am in sorrow. I am shaken by what I have done, or not done." On the other hand, the willingness to say it can lubricate the mechanisms by which we feel it. Nevertheless, I am not so much talking about what is not verbalized as about what is not internalized. I am talking about the person who says nothing because he feels nothing. Forgiveness can neither come to him nor grow from him because the soil of his soul is hardened by self-deception and self-satisfaction.

Which is precisely what it is. I have purposely avoided thus far the word "sin" because it is one of those code words which people prefer to react to rather than to think about. So choose your own word. Hold up whatever mirror you wish, provided you look at it without blinking. Perhaps it is the mirror of what your loved ones expect of you. Perhaps it is the mirror of what your religion beckons you to. Perhaps it is the mirror of your own loftiest expectations. Who, looking therein, can honestly say, "I am what I'm supposed to be"? Whitman once offered the poetic opinion that he "could turn and live with animals . . . so . . . self-contained," for, he rhapsodized,

> They do not sweat and whine about their condition;
> They do not lie awake in the dark and weep for their sins;
> They do not make me sick discussing their duty to God,
> Not one is dissatisfied . . . ("Song of Myself").

One hopes the poet noticed, however, that it was animals he was describing, not men. We ought not to feed on our need, but neither dare we ignore it. The need for forgiveness, given or received, realized or forgotten, is as universal as hunger.

II

If the ground of forgiveness is need, *the seed of forgiveness is love.*

Especially the love of God. I told earlier of my anger with certain doctrinal distortions that mess up men's lives. It is precisely at this point that such distortions occur; at the point, I mean, of the failure to take with radical seriousness the fact that God is love. That failure is often, though I think wrongly, read as being dominated by an Old Testament concept of God. This, I am confident, would have been news to Jesus, and bad news at that. After all, his God was an Old Testament God. The God of Jesus Christ and the God of some of his present-day misinterpreters bear only a faint family resemblance to each other, just as a cartoon caricature both resembles and distorts. Not that there are not things to distort. The Old Testament God is by turns remote and nearby, judicious and peevish, muscle-bulging and gentle. He walks in a garden, talks with his servants, calls up an army, strikes down an enemy, issues awkward orders, and makes impossible demands. But only an almost willful myopia can keep us from seeing that, over the long haul and *essentially,* the Old Testament God was good, gracious, loving, forgiving—fatherly.

Even if the Old Testament were to drop out of existence (as it practically has for many people), the New Testament should be enough to set us straight. God is father: this is its cry, its hope, and its crown. "Father" is the alpha and the omega of Jesus' ministry, literally: his first recorded word in the Temple, his last recorded word from the cross. In between, this is his story, this is his song: in the parable of the prodigal's waiting Father, in the hillside sermon, in the agony garden, in the skeins of compassion and the cords of mercy which bind them together and make them one—in all this, a father, forgiving and fulfilling.

So, don't you see, when you cry out, "But I don't deserve God's mercy!" you have accidentally defined that mercy? Mercy is precisely for the undeserving, for you, for me. Who *is* deserving? Who deserves any love he is proffered, for that matter? Are there not moments, however rare, when even the most imperceptive parent realizes that he does not deserve his children's love? Recall that word, early in the Gospel of Matthew (5:45), in which Jesus says that God makes his rain to fall upon the just and the unjust? That is usually taken to be a reference to the impartial *justice* of God. It now seems to me that it is an equally good description of the imperishable *love* of God. His mercy is given to the just and to the *unjust,* to the undeserving.

I freely admit that this emphasis upon the seeking mercy of God is but a fraction of the truth (a major fraction, I would contend, but still a fraction). Nevertheless, I have dealt with too many people who are torn, tortured, and terrified because they have heard only the minor fraction. It is time to recall and reiterate that the gospel is *Good* News, in spite of our badness. So I plead with you, especially with you who have been given a growling God, to remember the biblical promise—nay, more, the biblical *fact*—that his mercies are without number. "Beyond a wholesome discipline," in the words of the poet Ehrmann, "be gentle with yourself." [1] "Brightly beams our Father's mercy."

---

[1] "Desiderata" in *The Poems of Max Ehrmann* (Boston: Bruce Humphries).

III

The ground of forgiveness is need. The seed of forgiveness is love. *The moisture of forgiveness is fellowship.* Or, to put it another way, what brings the seed to flower is not retribution but restoration.

Consider a sample. Junior, a budding butler, is carrying the cream pitcher to the dining-room table (first mistake). He drops the pitcher atop your antique serving platter, breaking both (second and third mistakes). You shout (fourth mistake), "I've told you a thousand times not even to *touch* my crystal. Go to your room immediately." When your juvenile maitre d' gets to his room, what bothers him? Is it that he has been excluded from your dining room? Fat chance. He'd rather eat in the kitchen anyway, and besides there are toys in his room. What bothers him is that he has been shut out of the dining room of your affections. Being banned to a separate room is but tangible symbol of being banned from you. He is having a very elemental and human experience, the experience of separation, of estrangement, of alienation.

This is what cuts us up about the failure that calls forth the need for forgiveness. What distresses us is the emotional distance it causes, the painful gap it produces, the rooms of hurt and loneliness and hostility it banishes us to. This is why solitary confinement of a prisoner is among the more cruel and inhuman punishments that man's perversity has devised. One cannot reach out and touch another person, to feel the pulse of his hopes or fears, to hear the sounds of his hurts or happiness, to be strengthened by his joy, or even wounded by his rage.

Furthermore, as some people can sadly testify, this solitary cell of the self can be one in which a man feels himself locked away from God. The prisoner cries out, but, he fears, no one hears. He suffers, but no one cares. His life is loneliness wrapped in separation and sealed with fear. If this *is* one of the rooms in his Father's house, as Jesus promised, it must be in some remote wing long deserted and never visited by the Father.

Hence I said, a bit back, that forgiveness is restoration of fellowship. Consider the prodigal. Consider any marriage in which, though the people are living together, they have really separated. Then one forgiving day they come home—to each other. Consider the rediscovery of that godly love, godly because the Father's love will not let us go. Truly, merely "to forego resentment is a poor half forgiveness." [2] Forgiveness is not retribution, it is restoration. "We cannot hope to be instruments of God's peace when we ourselves are not at peace with others." [3]

This is much of the point of Paul's advice to the parish in Corinth. One of the members has offended against the peace and unity of that struggling little

[2] *The Interpreter's Bible* (Nashville: Abingdon Press, 1951), VII, 475a.

[3] Paton, *Instrument of Thy Peace*, p. 107.

church. He has apparently been disciplined. Now, Paul says to them, they should rather turn to forgive and encourage him lest he be overwhelmed by excessive sorrow (II Corinthians 2:7). So, Paul begs them, "reaffirm your love for him" (vs. 8). Show him this, plainly and publicly. Or, as Clarence Jordan translates it, "Go out of your way to show your love for him." Forgive him. Restore him to your midst in full fellowship.

It is the recognition of the necessity of such restoration which led me to say in an earlier book:

> For all the limitations of private confession I am nonetheless convinced that we could well take a page from the breviary of our brethren. We need *something* quite as specific as the confessional—in sin confessed, in forgiveness pronounced. I have often been almost covetous of my priest-brothers' capacity to send a penitent away—restored, renewed, and reconciled—with a convincing assurance which no pastoral counseling (particularly of the so-called "non-directive" sort) can either claim or accomplish.
>
> Let me illustrate. Some years ago a young woman came to me tortured with the guilt born with her illegitimate child, compounded by the cankerous secret kept even from the father of the child. I listened long. I spoke of what *I* knew of the forgiving grace of God. I wrapped both the time for speaking and the time for keeping silent in what *I* thought were the luminous, revealing veils of scripture, to no avail. Finally, moved by an unmistakable prompting, I took her to the chapel and knelt with her in prayer. Then I stood while she still knelt, placed my hand upon her head and said, "Rebecca" (this is, of course, not

her name), "Rebecca, I forgive you in the name of God. Now go, and live as a forgiven woman." [4]

The certainty of restoration is an indispensable part of forgiveness.

IV

If the ground of forgiveness is need, if the seed of forgiveness is love, if the moisture of forgiveness is fellowship, then finally *the flower of forgiveness is wholeness.*

As I wrote that sentence my plane was lowering into Dulles International Airport at Washington, D.C., Instantly my mind thought of some of the great names that have given stature and substance to our capital city's short but crowded history. As usual, I thought of Lincoln.

For some reason I also thought of Stanton, Lincoln's Secretary of War. I remembered how, before the President's election, Edwin Stanton had been one of Lincoln's most fierce opponents as well as one of his most unfair critics. He had called Lincoln a clown and a gorilla, had even permitted himself to wonder aloud why an expedition was being sent to Africa to search for a gorilla when there was a home-grown one in

[4] Ernest J. Fiedler and R. Benjamin Garrison, *The Sacraments: An Experiment in Ecumenical Honesty* (Nashville: Abingdon Press; Notre Dame, Indiana: Fides Press, 1969), p. 93.

Springfield, Illinois. Lincoln knew all this. He knew, too, that Stanton was the best man for this important post, so he appointed him to his war cabinet.

You say that Lincoln was only being politically astute? Quite possibly, though that interpretation does not disturb me. Indeed it is refreshing to discover a public figure who understood that politics and power can make a place for forgiveness. But I think it was more than prudence. It was heroic insight. "With malice toward none"—not even toward one's bitterest enemy. Surely it is an abiding testimony to the life-giving nature of forgiveness that it was this same Stanton who, with a heart no longer bitter but broken now, said at Lincoln's deathbed, "Now he belongs to the ages." As always, the healing power of forgiveness had flowed in both directions, making both men whole.

I conclude with two questions, far from rhetorical, and asked of and on behalf of all of us. The first question is John Donne's:

> "Wilt Thou forgive that sin, through which I run,
> And do run still, though still I do deplore?
> When Thou hast done, Thou hast not done,
> For I have more." *(Hymn to God the Father)*

The second question comes from the biographer of William Gladstone. Morley was commenting upon the Prime Minister's amazingly constructive handling of an extortioner and upon the public official's complete readiness to forgive. "There was no worldly wisdom in all this, we all know," he wrote. "But then," he added, "what are people Christians for?" [5]

"Wilt thou forgive?"

"What are people Christians for?"

"Lord, where there is injury let us sow pardon."

[5] John Morley, *The Life of William Ewart Gladstone* (New York: Macmillan, 1903), III, 419.

4

The Seed of Faith and Hope

*"where there is doubt, faith;
where there is despair, hope . . ."*

"For about thirty years I have been reading the Bible . . . , yet I am not so healed that I can . . . come to rest in the remedies God has pointed out to us." [1] The writer of those words, surprisingly, was Martin Luther. I say "surprisingly" because the great Reformer's very name has become almost synonymous with faith. With faith he lubricated the hinges of history and made them swing more freely than ever before. The whole life of this lovable, irritating German was, or at least seemed, what he himself called faith, a "yes of the heart," a

[1] *What Luther Says,* compiled by E. M. Plass (St. Louis: Concordia, 1959), Vol. I, #946.

conviction on which he staked his life,[2] "a living, daring confidence in the grace of God." [3] Yet the same man who said his yes, staked his life, and dared his confidence here confesses that faith was not uninterruptedly his.

Just so, our lives oscillate between faith and doubt, between hope and despair. To this extent Luther is Everyman. He interests us because he mirrors us. His holiness was worldly, as Francis said it should be, but it was not whole.

"O Lord," prayed the latter, "where there is doubt let me sow faith; where there is despair, hope."

I

Let it be understood that there is a necessary kind of doubt. There is, for instance, a methodological doubt about which I wrote in Chapter Two. I doubt in order to learn. Somebody asserts that water is comprised of particles of hydrogen and oxygen, or that you have to destroy a village in order to save it, or that you must burn down a university in order to build it. So you say, "Is that so? Let's see." You set about to examine the assertion, to challenge an axiom, in Einstein's phrase. That is, you doubt. Out of that doubt comes either the kind of clarity that gives you confidence or the kind

---

[2] *Ibid.*, #1376.
[3] *Ibid.*, #1491.

of confusion that indicates that you need to do some more thoughtful doubting.

Likewise there is a necessary kind of religious doubt without which faith is bogus. Some pretty stupid things can be asserted in the name of religion. Unless you are willing to take them with a grain of salt, which is to say unless you are unwilling to take them at all without examining them, your faith may be full, but the question is, Full of what? The Spanish philosopher Unamuno said that "Don Juan never questioned the dogma of the church in which he was brought up because he never seriously considered them." [4] Ouch. Dante gave us the reassuring warning: "At the very root of truth will spring offshoots of doubt." [5] There is, then, a necessary kind of doubt.

But there is also a necessarily destructive kind of doubt. It splits the doubter down the center. It immobilizes the fractions of the man remaining. It renders him indecisive and afraid. Somebody once defined a liberal as a chap who doubts his premises even while he is proceeding upon them. But the kind of destructive doubt I have in mind here makes him incapable of proceeding on his premises, or upon any other ones, for that matter.

So, on the one hand, there should be no limitation

---

[4] *Perplexities and Paradoxes* (New York: Philosophical Library, 1945), p. 123.

[5] *Divine Comedy,* Canto 4.

whatever to what we may doubt. Nothing is intellectually off limits. On the other hand, our doubt should be carried out in such a way as to make possible a decision. We doubt for an outcome. Doubt is a jury, but it must eventually be required to bring in a verdict.

Somewhere the silly idea got started that faith equals certainty, that doubt equals uncertainty, and never the twain shall meet. If so, Jesus of Nazareth was a colossal failure as a man of faith. He constantly faced decisions about his own nature, about his own mission, and about his own life, in which urgency combined with ambiguity. For instance, he achieved "no mathematical certainty of his messiahship (but that) lack of certainty was no barrier to his complete obedience." [6] Certainly, then, the "Christian will not require his own obedience to God to be held in suspense to a test of certainty which Jesus did not even require of himself." [7]

You may have noticed that I have been using the word "doubt" here in two related but quite different meanings. To doubt the composition of H_2O is a very different matter from doubting the makeup of messiahship, discipleship, integrity, or personality. Life will wait while we decide what water is and will reward our search with certitude. Life will not wait while we decide what life is and will reward our search with ambiguity. Life's laboratory is open twenty-four hours a day; its

---

[6] Carl Michalson, *The Rationality of Faith* (New York: Scribner's, 1963), p. 79.

[7] *Ibid.*

lab reports are always marked, "experiment incomplete." Certainty is precluded. Finality is impossible. Doubt springs eternal in the human breast.

Some people simply cannot endure life on the knife-edge of doubt and so fall into despair. The word "despair," the dictionary indicates, comes from a Middle English root meaning "to be shorn of all hope." Anyway, whether this is its linguistic rootage or not, it is its living, deadly result. Despair is by no means "the terribly easy way out" [8] as Kierkegaard mistakenly said. It is not easy to thrash about in forty fathoms with no shore in sight. It is not easy to cry out with not even an echo for answer and with the fear that none is there to hear. It is not easy to have a life full of everything except meaning, a life well-fed but hungry, well-read but ignorant, well-paid but poor. Despair is a kind of pernicious anemia of the spirit, characterized by a dangerously decreasing supply of the life-giving cells of hope.

Note, though, that despair and anxiety are not interchangeable terms or equivalent conditions. Tillich says that Jesus Christ is that figure in whom all forms of anxiety are present but in whom all forms of despair are absent. Anxiety is a universal human state based upon the inescapable fact that the human mind is "a permanent factory of fears" [9]—fears of what I cannot do (called

---

[8] *Journal* (London: Oxford University Press, 1938), #1030.

[9] *The Courage to Be*, p. 39.

finitude), fears of what I cannot believe (called doubt), fears of what I cannot escape (called guilt). Anxiety of this sort is no more separable from life than wetness is separable from water.

Despair is a beast of a different genre. Despair is anxiety crystallized into permanence and internalized into darkness. You cannot dissolve despair in a solution of good advice or melt it down on the Bunsen burner of the good old college try. It yields to no "Damn Yankee" optimism—as well tell a legless man to run as counsel a despairing one that he's "gotta have heart." You cannot lift yourself by your bootstraps if you have no boots.

II

Into the midst of such starkness, darkness, and emptiness the saintly petition of our prayer shines like a million candles in a single room: "where there is doubt let us sow faith; where there is despair, hope."

Few words in the language of religion cry out for as much semantic purging as the word "faith" (Tillich). The New Testament itself is not of one mind about its meaning, using the word in a confusing variety of ways. Sometimes it means to believe that something is a fact, i.e., I believe that the Beatitudes are from the lips of Jesus. Sometimes it means to assent to the truth of something, i.e., I believe that the peacemakers are the sons of God. Sometimes it means to trust, especially to trust a person, i.e., I trust my life to the Man from Nazareth who gave us the Beatitudes. Then there is that more inclusive usage, "the Faith," something coterminous with all that Christianity is.

Francis intends us to be praying for a very comprehensive thing here when he uses the word "faith." It is a blend of the New Testament meanings discussed above. It is not a cold acceptance or a dispassionate assent to this or that truth. To take an analogy: it is not very useful to speak abstractly of love. One needs to know who loves whom and how. Likewise, it is not very useful to speak abstractly of faith. One needs to know who believes what and how, or better, who trusts whom and why. The Hebrew word for trust (batah) basically means "to throw oneself forward" in unqualified abandon. *To have faith in the biblical sense is not merely to assent with one's mind but to respond with one's life.* Moreover "to all who received him, . . . he gave power to become" (John 1:12).

Back in the seventeenth century a great scientist and theologian, Blaise Pascal, likened faith to a cosmic card game in which the stakes are high, the risks great, the outcome uncertain, but the game necessary. Our comparing faith to a celestial poker game might make our Puritan ancestors spin in their graves. But after they had stripped the comparison of its imagery, I rather suspect that they would agree with it. For faith is not a game of solitaire in which one can shuffle through the deck, cheat a little, and make it come out right every time.

Faith is a mighty venture, a terribly crucial game in which one stakes one's life.

Likewise Christian hope, like Christian faith, is not quite hope in the ordinary sense of the word. ("I hope it won't rain," I say, with rain clouds overhead. Or "I hope I'll ace this exam," I dream, not having cracked the textbook in months.) On the contrary Christian hope, because it is bound to what God is and has promised to do, is an "assured hope," as Mr. Lincoln said in another connection. It is assured in the same sense that an insurance policy is—underwritten by God's sure word, a hope intact because the premiums have been paid in advance (though, by a gracious reversal, the premiums have been paid by God). Because what he said in Christ is what he is in fact, our hope is not sent empty away.

It is not accidental, I judge, that Francis placed the words "faith" and "hope" one on top of the other in this prayer. One cannot instill faith without arousing hope. Conversely, hopelessness is a skinny symptom of a starving faith. This is beautifully illustrated by a possibly apocryphal but nonetheless true story from the life of Luther. In one of his periods of giantesque discouragement, he saw his wife come down to breakfast one day dressed in black clothes of mourning, as if about to attend a funeral. When the downcast pastor asked his wife what on earth she was doing, she replied softly, "Mourning the death of God." "Where there is doubt, faith; where there is despair, hope."

III

Finally, "Grant that we may not so much seek to be consoled as to console."

"Let not your hearts be troubled" counseled Jesus (John 14:1a). Why not? the disciples might well have asked, considering all that lay ahead for him and for themselves. For him: that lonely garden across the Kidron Valley wherein he prayed and struggled with such passion and pain that it was as if he had lost great quantities of blood; a dear and impulsive friend profanely denying their friendship; the last mile walk to the place of execution; the nails and the sword; the crowd's jeers and his mother's tears—all of this yet ahead. And for them: the suffocating knowledge that they slept while he suffered and that they fled while he bled. Surely it took either a lot of nerve or a lot of trust to say, under these doomful circumstances, "Let not your hearts be troubled."

It also took a lot of honesty. At the very least, it should remind *us* that the Lord offered no Pollyanna promise that the worst we fear will not happen. It just may. At least it did happen to him and to them, and may to you and to me.

Notice, too, that the prayer does not say that it is wrong to want to be consoled, merely that you should not want it *so much* as to console. Of the two, to be consoled may be the more difficult. It requires acknowledging your need. It is hard on the pride. It does violence to our fiercely protected streak of Yankee independence. Yet when our time to be comforted comes, as come it will to every person, it would be pridefully wrong to keep another from giving.

The crucial contrast caught in the clauses of this prayer is symbolized and summarized in two documents recently coming to my notice.

The first, oddly, is a government document. A few years ago one of Scotland's historic houses was offered for sale in the United Kingdom Information Office's *News from Scotland* (August, 1949). The name of the mansion was "Castle Gloom," located in the village of Dollar, once spelled Dolour, or sorrow. The place names there are burred with sadness. Castle Gloom was so called until 1490 when the Duke of Argyle changed it to Castle Campbell. A century and a half later (1644) the castle was sacked and burned by the Royalist army of Montrose. If you had lived in the fifteenth century and had wanted to send a letter to someone residing in that old house, you would have addressed it as follows:

Castle of Gloom
In the Parish of Dolour (Sorrow)
Beside the Water of Grief
In the Glen of Care[10]

Many people in our midst can be found at that address, even today.

---

[10] For this citation I am indebted to David A. MacLennan, *Entrusted with the Gospel* (Philadelphia: Westminster Press, 1956), p. 105.

The second document, equally oddly, is the report of a search from an abstract office. A New York lawyer whose client was purchasing a tract of land in New Orleans objected because the abstract of title did not show any matters prior to 1803 and demanded that the title previous to this time be traced. The seller's attorney, an old Louisiana lawyer, replied as follows:

> I was unaware that any educated man in the world failed to know that Louisiana was purchased from France in 1803. The title to the land was acquired by France by right of conquest from Spain. The land came into possession of Spain by right of discovery made in 1492 by a sailor named Christopher Columbus, who had been granted the privilege of seeking a new route to India by the then reigning monarch, Isabella. The good queen, being a pious woman [and as careful about titles, almost I might say, as you] took the precaution of securing the blessing of the Pope for the voyage before she sold her jewels to help Columbus. Now the Pope, as you know, is the emissary of Jesus Christ, the Son of God, and God, it is commonly accepted, made the world. Therefore, I believe it is safe to presume that He also made that part of the world called Louisiana, and I hope that now you are satisfied.

The contrast between those two documents is a bit whimsical to be sure. But between the Castle of Gloom with its ultimate despair and the ownership of the earth with its ultimate faith in the God who created it in the first place lies a world of Christian difference. In such a world faith can outdistance doubt and hope can outlive despair. In such a world we can with confidence pray,

"Lord, make us instruments of thy peace.
Where there is doubt, let us sow faith,
Where there is despair, hope; . . .
O Divine Master,
Grant that we may not so much
Seek to be consoled as to console."

Amen.

5
The Seed of Joy

"where there is darkness, light;
where there is sadness, joy.
Grant that we may not so much seek to be understood
As to understand."

Henry J. Hobson, Protestant Episcopal Bishop of Cincinnati, once referred to the fact that the flag of the United Kingdom is flown at Buckingham Palace only when the sovereign is there. The bishop then added that joy is the flag that the Christian displays when Christ the King is in residence.

This chapter is about joy, a quality of life easy to choose but seemingly easier to lose. The thesis of what follows can be quite simply stated, although not without accusing me and people like me for permitting the juices of joy to drain from their days. I want to suggest, because the Christian gospel insists, that *a man's joy in life is an accurate measure of his confidence in God.* When Phillips Brooks was asked, "Why your optimism?" he responded, "Because I am a Christian."

"O Lord, make us instruments of *thy* peace. Where there is sadness, let us sow joy, where there is darkness, light. O Divine Master, grant that we may not so much seek to be understood as to understand."

I

Luther observes somewhere that all despair is of the devil. We do not believe in the devil anymore. That's just the devil of it. Somebody, however, is doing business at the same old stand. There is something satanic, something anti-God and anti-godly, about that failure of nerve and that collapse of confidence which drops us into despair. I have in my library a volume entitled *A Handbook of Christian Theology*. Mistitled, I should say, for it has no article on joy. You can no more write a Christian theology without reference to joy than you can write a physics textbook without reference to energy. The phrase "joyless Christian life" is bluntly a contradiction in terms. It is like speaking of mindless thinking or heartless feeling or round rectangles.

I wonder why we have thought we could cut joy from the Christian life without fatally injuring both. I am not sure, but I offer a guess. Consider for example what has happened to words like "pleasure," "happiness," "zest," "glee," "gaiety," or even "fun." To how many people would it occur to describe the Christian life in these terms? Is it not regretfully true that we can point to too few zestful, gleeful Christians? On the contrary, it has been charged (and too accurately I fear) that Christianity is the enemy of pleasure, the adversary of gaiety, and the death of fun., So when Jesus promises his people a hearty, overflowing joy which no one can steal from them (John 16:22, 24), few people take him seriously, partly because too few Christians have.

On the other hand, it is very dangerous to *equate* joy with happiness. In the previous chapter I tried to draw a distinction between anxiety and despair. Now I must try to draw a different kind of distinction between happiness and joy. Happiness is ephemeral, joy is enduring. Happiness is the frosting on the cake; joy is the salt on the steak. Happiness depends upon changing circumstances; joy depends upon unchanging confidence. After Frank Costello, the gangland leader and con man, had been sentenced for perjury, a reporter asked him if he was unhappy about the decision. He replied, "I have never been unhappy." Right. He had probably never been joyful either. Happiness is like the dew in all its passing beauty; joy is like the ocean in all its surging strength.

Christian joy, however, is something considerably more than this. That "considerably more" is unforgettably expressed in the theme song of the folk album "Joy Is Like the Rain":

> "I saw raindrops on my window:
> Joy is like the rain.

Laughter runs across my pane,
Joy is like the rain . . .

I saw Christ in wind and thunder:
Joy is tried by storm,
Christ asleep within my bode,
Whipped by wind yet still abroad:
Joy is tried by storm . . ." [1]

It is surely significant that the composer of this song, Sister Miriam Therese Winter, is a member of a religious society (The Medical Mission Sisters) which cares for the sick in the great need areas of the world, as a work of Christian charity.

Christian joy is a steady confidence and even a heady exaltation in what God has promised and presented in Christ. In Elizabeth Goudge's superb novel of Cromwellian Britain, *The Child From the Sea,* an exiled clergyman, in a fit of discouragement, laments, "Faith and depression were not mutually destructive for faith could be carried . . . in a dark lantern, but one missed the glow." [2] Unhappiness may hamper but cannot undo it. Happiness may approximate but cannot express it. Crucifixion may threaten but cannot destroy it. Its base is above itself. Its bond is beyond itself. Its guarantor is God.

---

[1] Words from Joy Is Like the Rain by Sister Miriam Therese Winter © MCMLXV by Medical Mission Sisters. Reprinted by permission of Vanguard Music Corp., 250 West 57th St., New York, N.Y. Original recording available on album AVS 101 from Avant Garde Records Inc. All rights for Canada controlled by Chappell & Co. Limited Toronto.

[2] (New York: Coward-McCann, 1970), p. 557.

> It is interesting to recall that the most rollicking organ music old periwig Bach ever wrote is not dedicated to the joy of tobacco (although he did that) or coffee (and he praised that) or the inventiveness among his fellow musicians, nor dedicated to the levity of the Count of Brandenburg—but *In Dir ist Freude* (In Thee is Joy)! [8]

Few ways of seeing what the Christian faith can mean are better than through the eyes of the newly converted Christian. A few years ago a young woman rushed up to me after Sunday worship and cried, "It's Pentecost! Pentecost! Don't these people know what that means? It means the Spirit of God has come to us—the Spirit of *God* has come to *us*." Who was this eager enthusiast? She had been born and reared a Jew. She had sung enough of old Bach's music with our choir to be touched by his joy and moved by his message. That particular morning she had sung to a congregation that seemed to her lethargic, predictable, and detached rather than enthusiastic, spontaneous, and involved. She was commenting upon our joy, or rather upon our sad and saddening lack of it. She had recently embraced a gospel that the preacher called Good News. But our hymns did not sound like it, and our eyes did not look like it. The joyful tides of our worship had been reduced to a mighty squirt gun.

---

[8] Joseph Sittler in the sermon "The Care of the Earth" in *Sermons to Intellectuals*, ed. F. Littell (New York: Macmillan, 1963), p. 24.

So mark it down as plain: we have as much joy as we have faith. A deficiency in the one marks a failure in the other. It was not without reason that Francis counseled us to expand the acreage and increase the yield of men's joy.

II

Now I want to ask you to shift gears with me and to synchromesh your attention with that closely linked petition, "where there is darkness, let us sow light."

It is not shedding light into darkness to continue to build an economy so dependent upon armaments that even the most optimistic social analysts are pessimistic about what will happen when we can no longer count upon the built-in stimulus of blood and destruction.

It is not shedding light into darkness to break a druggist's or a bookseller's store windows simply because other businessmen who are armaments manufacturers are in town attempting to recruit employees. Nor, need I add, is it shedding light into darkness to ignore the violence from which the recruiting firm is making millions.

It is not shedding light into darkness to quash the sober recommendations of university administrators and to prevent even stupid speeches from being heard.

It is not shedding light into darkness to suppose that a bleeding head should not be bandaged if the brain inside that head thinks differently from yours. (One of the more colorful trustees of the church I serve offered the following resolution during a period of "campus unrest": "Be it known that all plutocrats, pigs, long hairs, squares, and other assorted dingalings can expect to have oil and wine poured into their wounds at this church." His language was perhaps a trifle picturesque, but he had certainly read, and understood, the New Testament!)

It is not shedding light into darkness to state opinions as facts nor to print them without substantiation.

It is not shedding light into darkness to repeat base and baseless rumors.

It is not shedding light into darkness to treat gossip like gospel or gospel like gossip.

It is not shedding light into darkness to make anonymous phone calls.

It is not shedding light into darkness to judge a man by his appearance, whether the color of his skin, the length or distribution of his hair, or the cut or type of his uniform.

It is not shedding light into darkness to desecrate the judicial processes, whether from the judge's bench, the prisoner's dock, the attorney's desk, or the jury's box.

It is not shedding light into darkness to let labels divide or fears unite.

And above all, it is not shedding light into darkness—indeed it is doubling that darkness—when, seeing these things happen, you let fear curb and curtail your candor or control and silence your tongue.

III

Edward B. Lytton has said that "the classic literature is always modern." I am struck again and again by that mark of the classic, and especially of this classic prayer.

At this point in the history of this nation and of the church the most important phrase may be the Franciscan petition, "O Divine Master, grant that we may not so much seek to be understood as to understand."

In moments of discouragement it is temptingly easy to cry out, with more than a tinge of self-pity, "But why can't they understand? Why do people believe the most casual lunacy they read in the newspaper but resist the most obvious application of what they read in the New Testament? Why are political, social, or vocational ties more binding than religious ones? Why cannot Christians, at least, trust one another?"

But, if Francis is right, that terribly easy way is the wrong one. The harder petition, the rougher road, is the prayer "not so much to be understood as to understand."

It is not easy to understand the patent human preference for property rights over personal rights, nor the convenient inconsistency that deplores broken windows in American cities but justifies devastated villages in Vietnam. Not easy—but imperative.

It is not easy to understand the pent-up frustrations that cause people to hurl bricks and insults and to invite the very confrontations they claim to deplore. Not easy—but imperative.

Milton once said, speaking of truth: "Let her and falsehood grapple; whoever knew truth put to the worse in a free and open encounter?" It is not easy to understand men, whether of the right or of the left, who are so intellectually timid that they will do anything to prevent or control such an encounter. Not easy —but imperative.

It is not easy to understand those who would limit compassion to their own kind—limit and thus destroy it. Not easy—but imperative.

It is not easy to understand the fear and the insecurity that make well-meaning and otherwise likeable people so distrust themselves and you that they will not speak their piece to your face. But they *are* insecure, they *are* afraid. They *do* see something in you and in me that they do not trust. Though it is difficult to understand why, it is imperative.

It is not easy to understand either contempt of court or a contemptuous court—but, before it is too late, we had better try.

It is not easy to understand the way in which even Christians can value opinions more highly than persons and thus can divide themselves from those who name a common Lord. It is not easy but positively necessary. "O Lord, grant that we may not so much seek to be understood as to understand."

Look at how these three petitions tie together. The kind of joy I am talking about is deep and essentially indestructible. It survives discouragements because it is based in a basic confidence in God and is expressed through a steady obedience to him. To put it in a way that I trust the reader will understand even though it is paradoxical, it is sometimes possible and occasionally necessary to be both unhappy and joyful.

Such joy sheds light, not least because it beams forth from One who called himself the Light of the World. It—or rather he—exposes evil wherever or in whomever found. He sometimes heals, sometimes burns, sometimes warms, sometimes nourishes, sometimes judges. But this light shines, everlastingly.

Because it shines, it understands; that is, it stands under all that we are or fail to be. This prayer of St. Francis, profoundly prayed and inly appropriated, makes newborn sense of much that otherwise is chaotic and collision-bound. When you see a person—a *person* —you begin to understand him. When you begin to understand him, you find it more difficult to dismiss him. Then, it may be, you will discover that you love him.

What I have written in this chapter expresses—or at least intends—a compassion that has no *human* limit, a love that aches to be lived—in you, through you, and for you—a joyful, enlightening, and understanding task.

6
The Seed of Benevolence

J. D. Salinger has an amusing but also poignant and revealing passage in one of his stories. He says:

> When Seymour and I were fifteen and thirteen, we came out of our room one night to listen, I believe, to Stoopnagle and Budd on the radio. . . . There were only three people present—our father, our mother, and our brother Waker. . . . Waker—who was at that instant according to my figures, almost exactly nine years and fourteen hours old—was standing near the piano, in his pajamas, barefooted, with tears streaming down his face. . . . That morning, as we already knew, Waker and Walt had been given matching, beautiful, well-over-the-budget birthday presents—two red-and-white striped, double-barred twenty-six-inch bicycles. . . . About ten minutes before Seymour and I came out of the bedroom, Les had found out that Waker's bicycle wasn't safely stored in the basement of our apartment building with Walt's. That afternoon in

Central Park Waker had given his away. An unknown boy ("some schnook he never saw before in his life") had come up to Waker and asked him for his bicycle, and Waker had handed it over. Neither Les nor Bessie, of course, was unmindful of Waker's "very nice, generous intentions," but both of them also saw the details of the transaction with an implacable logic of their own. What, substantially, they felt that Waker should have done . . . was to give the boy a nice, long *ride* on the bicycle. Here Waker broke in, sobbing. The boy didn't *want* a nice, long ride, he wanted the *bicycle*. He'd never had one, the boy; he'd always *wanted* one. . . . I won't describe in detail (for once) how Seymour . . . competently blundered his way to the heart of the matter so that, a few minutes later, the three belligerents actually kissed and made up. My real point here is a blatantly personal one, and I think I've already stated it.[1]

I have recently plunked down the wherewithal to purchase for one of my offspring a beautiful, well-over-the-budget, green-and-white striped, single-barred, five-speed Schwinn racing bike. So I rush right on to observe, for the benefit of panicky parents, that it is not necessary to take Salinger's story with more literalness than many moderns accord the Holy Scriptures. The old folk motto is really wrong: it is *both* the spirit and the gift that count. I merely mean to stress that Salinger's story has caught some of that pristine enthusiasm, spontaneity, and self-forgetfulness which the New Tes-

---

[1] *Raise High the Roof Beam, Carpenters* and *Seymour, An Introduction* (Boston: Little, Brown, 1955), pp. 238-41.

tament meant when it said that God loves a hilarious giver (II Corinthians 9:7). For, as Francis reminds us, also echoing the New Testament, "it is in giving that we receive."

I

It is altogether appropriate that we should test this theorem to see how it proves out in the ministry of Jesus.

He stated it rather more positively than a theory, of course. He stated it dogmatically:

> Give, and it will be given to you; good measure, pressed down, shaken together, running over, will be put into your lap. For the measure you give will be the measure you get back (Luke 6:38).
>
> The man who has found his own life will lose it, but the man who has lost it for my sake will find it (Matthew 10:39, Phillips).

Then this, with a slight variation in theme: "freely ye have received, freely give" (Matthew 10:8a KJV). These are only a slight sampling. Jesus described our living in terms of giving.

Moreover, the New Testament recalls, Jesus not only commended the way of giving, he walked it. He begrudged neither time nor strength. Was it a dubiously honest public official named Zacchaeus, treed by his own tawdry business ethics yet yearning to be freed? Probably Jesus did not have the time, but he *made* the time, he *gave* the time to go home with the little guy and break bread with him and show him a more excellent way.

Was it a Samaritan woman of dubious personal ethics, conspicuously pausing beside a public well? It was a hot day, and the Teacher was probably already tired. Nevertheless he summoned both the insight and the dedicated carelessness to talk to a woman of that reputation and of that race. Ungrudgingly.

Was it a soldier, whose very uniform advertised a hated conqueror and symbolized a hateful cause? Yes it was, but no matter—the officer's child was ill and needed a physician. So Jesus gave.

Attention is often and understandably paid to the fact that Jesus gave his life at the last. However, that final, faithful giving on Golgotha was but the climax of a lifetime of smaller, daily gifts, each one including the essential ingredient of himself. The Cross was the supreme, but not the solitary, example of this giving.

Quite naturally, therefore, those who remembered and reverenced his life recorded it in the New Testament in these consistently giving terms. We hear this accent in a passage from I Peter:

> Who, when he was reviled, reviled not again; when he suffered, he threatened not; but committed himself to him that judgeth righteously: Who his own self bare our sins in his own body on the tree, that we, being dead to sins, should live unto righteousness: by whose stripes ye were healed. For ye were as sheep going astray; but are now returned unto the Shepherd and Bishop of your souls (I Peter 2:23-25 KJV).

These words from the New Testament in turn reverberate with messianic music from the prophet Isaiah:

> His visage was so marred more than any man. . . . He is despised and rejected of men; a man of sorrows, and acquainted with grief: . . . and we esteemed him not. Surely he hath borne our griefs, and carried our sorrows. . . . But he was wounded for our transgressions, he was bruised for our iniquities . . . and with his stripes we are healed. . . . He was oppressed, and he was afflicted, yet he opened not his mouth: he is brought as a lamb to the slaughter. . . . For the transgression of my people he was stricken. And he made his grave with the wicked, and with the rich in his death. . . . He shall see of the travail of his soul, and shall be satisfied. (Selections from chapters 52 and 53 KJV)

Arising out of this moving but long-neglected passage in the Old Testament, and apparently out of Jesus' own understanding of his role and mission, the New Testament affirms that our Lord took "the form of a servant" (Philippians 2:7). The word "form," we should note, can be used in two quite different ways. Form can equal appearance: a man's words have the form of sincerity, the implication being that the man beneath the words is insincere. Or form can equal reality, as the perfect form of a race horse, the implication being that it *is* perfect. When we are told that Jesus took the form of a servant, this does not mean that he merely appeared this way. He was no God with a human mask. He was no sham servant. A mother who weeps *in order to* move her children to mend their ways will leave them unmoved, for tears come not from the eyes but from the heart. So when Jesus took the form of a servant, he was not playing a role but displaying a reality.

Thus he "humbled himself" (Philippians 2:8a). Yet, as we have already observed, that humiliating death on a cross was only the full and final form of the life that led him there. Jesus could have said, as Paul did, "I die daily" (I Corinthians 15:31 KJV). He died a little when he saw men wound themselves with faithless, fretful worries about "tomorrow and tomorrow and tomorrow." He suffered when he heard them express hot anger at sins but cold contempt for sinners. He died a little more when his words were admired but not heeded, when his deeds were advertised but not duplicated, when his God was studied but not served. The last nail pierced him to a cross on Calvary, but they had tried to kill him after his very first sermon. And all the years between they had been forging and driving the nails, day by day, deed by deed, failure by failure.

Yet in the midst of all this he continued to give. So it was that his own words came true in his own life. Recall them again: "give, and it will be given to you, good measure, pressed down, shaken together, running over, will be put into your lap."

Consider how fully that was true of him. He who sought no name but servant has been given "a name which is above every name." He cried out, "He who believes in me, believes not in me but in him who sent me" (John 12:44). Yet men *have believed and do believe* in him as well as in the God who sent him. He who was willing to be cast into the most terrible darkness has been the wellspring of the most revealing light. The cup of his life, so early ended and so gladly given away, has been refilled to overflowing.

So it was this Life, this instrument of God's peace, who taught Francis to pray, and the ages to understand, that "it is in giving that we receive."

II

We have just observed that Jesus of Nazareth taught the ages to understand this truth. I suppose, though, that we have honestly to admit that we have not really understood it until, like our Lord, we have actually undergirded it with our own lives.

That, anyhow, is what Peter seemed to be feeling toward when, way back near the beginning of the church, he wrote, "To this you have been called, because Christ also suffered for you, leaving you an example, that you should follow in his steps" (I Peter 2:21). Note: "leaving you an example, that you should follow."

I delight in a story coming out of the life of that old Socialist warrior, Norman Thomas. His friends and opponents were giving him a testimonial dinner—his friends because they feared, and his opponents because they hoped, that he was going to retire from public life. All kinds of people were there, among them those who had fought Thomas every step of the way, those who thought that his ideas were naïve at best and dangerous at worst. He had long been engaged in dubious battle for many radical causes. He thought that women should have the right to vote and that workmen should have a voice in the circumstances of their toil. He had other clearly "revolutionary" aims. Anyway, they had now gathered to tell him what a great guy he was. Thomas listened to their speeches with wry amusement and probably with not a little disbelief. Then he was called upon to respond. He rose and began his speech with this rapier-like thrust, "Ladies and gentlemen," he said. "I would gladly trade all of this admiration for a little support."

I wonder sometimes whether the Master, hovering over our history, does not feel more than a little like that. He came not to be admired but to be followed—leaving us an example. We may, if we wish, "crown him with many crowns" so long as we remember that the real jewels in his diadem are the deeds that duplicate, or anyway approximate, his own.

Note, too, that the saintly admonition of our prayer is not that we should give *in order to* receive. That, I suspect, is the way we often misread it: honesty is the best policy. That is, it is politic and profitable. "Kill them with kindness." Be nice to the nasty old woman across the street, so that the old bat will have to recognize what a fine chap you really are!

No, Jesus was laboring for, and Francis was praying for, something considerably more direct and considerably less calculating than that. They were simply elucidating a law of life. They were commenting upon a causal connection. They were saying, "Life tends to give back what you pour into it." Frown, and life will scowl back. Seek revenge, and you will be wounded by the angry edge of your own dagger. Major in condemnation, and you will invite your own. On the other hand, to give forgiveness is to increase both the capacity and the likelihood of receiving it. Goodwill multiplies itself. Compassion duplicates itself. Usually you get back what you give.

Further on the positive side, the beauty of this promise is that its fulfillment does not depend upon your capacity to give *perfectly*. Consider, for instance, your capacity to give understanding. Recently a quite perceptive and highly intelligent young woman said to me, "My parents do not really understand me, but they're really trying to—and that's what counts." Don't you see? This *is* what counts. She was commenting, admiringly, not upon their competence—parents are by definition incompetent—but upon their compassion. Emerson says it similarly in his essay on "Gifts": "The only gift is a portion of thyself." That, this young woman was saying, is what my parents are trying to give. That, finally, is what counts. The gift without the giver *is* bare. The most paltry gift plus the giver is a richness beyond compare.

Some have no doubt noted that I have written this prayer of St. Francis in the plural, not the singular—"Lord, make us," not "Lord, make me" instruments. This is because of the growing and, for me, inescapable conviction that most of the important truths of the

Christian life are corporate. Therefore, the observation that giving precedes getting has something to say to the church. It is terribly easy for the church to be so protective of her own life that she loses it, in every wrong and wronging sense.[2] I sat quietly by recently while our Administrative Board reluctantly cut more than 10 percent out of our budget. I found myself wondering how we would explain to shut-ins that after that they might no longer hear our services broadcast. I wondered whether the congregation I serve really wished to say to our theological schools that, while of course we would rather like to have a pastor or so in the future, we could not bear any more of the cost of educating them. I wondered whether we really were so poor that job training for blacks would have to be placed beyond our ken or compassion. With each stroke of the fiscal pen, I kept hearing a haunting warning, "They who seek, lose; they who give, gain."

As I reflect upon the people who have influenced my life, it is accusingly clear that they have been those who have learned and shared the grace of giving. My mother often blames my bad teeth on the fact that she lived on a graduate school diet of Hershey bars and bananas during the pregnancy that resulted in my birth. Maybe so, but she gave me some things a lot more important than strong teeth. My other parents gave me a

---

[2] I have developed this theme more fully in *Portrait of the Church—Warts and All*, especially in Chapter 7. (Nashville: Abingdon Press, 1964).

wife who is probably the most unselfish person I shall ever know. My children give an affection and a loyalty beyond any possible paternal deserving. Not long ago I drove over into Indiana and had lunch with my old English professor of college days, a dear, devoted autocrat who gave good lectures, bad grades—and herself—to her students. I think, too, of friends who have been willing to give, and to accept, both faithfulness and frailty, far beyond the borders of caution, the boundaries of compassion, or the margins of restraint. All of these—parents, family, teachers, friends—have given beyond their resources and thus have called me beyond mine. They have taught me, however imperfectly, that to give is to receive.

I think it was Ernest Hemingway who gave the medal of his Nobel prize for literature to a church in Santiago. For, he said, "You really do not feel you own something until you can give it away."

That, I judge, is what Jesus has been trying to tell us for twenty centuries, and Francis for seven: you do not really possess anything—including yourself—until you give it away." "It is in giving that we receive."

7
The Seed of Life

"It is in dying that we are born to eternal life."

One of the interesting and portentous discussions among medical people has to do with the question, When is an individual dead, medically speaking? Pistol quite confidently assured Shakespeare's Falstaff that the old king was dead as a doornail. But if he could have had a little modern medical advice, and especially some of the sophisticated equipment which medical technology has developed, he might not have been quite so sure. A death certificate used to be issued after a stethoscope had been placed to the chest and no heartbeat detected. Nowadays, however, the heart can be kept beating by artificial means long after it is able to beat on its own. As a result, complicated readings of the brain waves are more usually employed as the final criterion for determining that death has occurred.

The ancients, including our primitive biblical ancestors, identified life with the blood, quite understandably. They observed that, when a man lost his blood, he died. So with a crude logic characteristic of animistic religions they concluded that life was *in* the blood. (As the book of Leviticus puts it, "the life of the flesh is in the blood" [17:11a].) This is one of the reasons for the widespread biblical imagery of blood and sacrifice, which imagery most moderns find so unsatisfactory if not downright repulsive. In almost all cases, however, if you will simply substitute the word "life" for the word "blood" you will have a clearer notion of the intended meaning: The life of Jesus Christ—freely given up—cleanses us.

An implication of this is that, if death is difficult to define with precision, its counterpart, life, is even more elusive.

All of this is admittedly a rather ponderous introduction to the fact that words like "death" and "life" have double, and sometimes even multiple meanings. Thus as we contemplate this final phrase in the prayer of St. Francis it is important to be clear in what sense we are using these words, "It is in dying that we are born to eternal life."

I

It is abundantly evident that the gospel of Jesus and the gospel about Jesus take both life and death with high seriousness.

The New Testament is saying that the two, life and death, go together and one's understanding of the one is affected by his understanding of the other. If we lived in a land where the sun always shone, or never shone, it is doubtful whether terms like "light" or "darkness" would even exist, let alone make any sense. The one is, and is meaningful, only over against the other. Simon and Garfunkel's phrase, "The Sounds of Silence," communicates beautifully to us only because we have known both sounds and silence. The one is defined in terms of the other. Just so, life is precious because death is inevitable. The death rate stands stubbornly at 100 percent, despite the skill of the physican, despite the cosmetics of the mortician, despite the circumlocutions of language, despite the yearnings of the human heart.

The Bible holds both of these facts, of life and of death, in one inclusive embrace. It is neither dazzled by life nor intimidated by death. "If a man die . . ." cries the book of Job (14:14). Ah, but there is no "if" about it. Jesus wept at the tomb of his dead friend, Lazarus, unwilling to dodge and unable to escape the cold fact. The man was dead. No euphemistic evasion there—not "passed away" to "the sweet by and by" but quite literally and quite completely dead. In this attitude Jesus simply is being a realistic son of Abraham. The Bible does not dwell on death. It uses no italics or red ink or banner headlines. It just quietly assumes and therefore faces the fact of death.

It is because of this unblinking candor about death

that its gospel of life has any right to be heard. The credentials of courage are most convincing when presented by men who have known fear. What the gospel seeks to affirm about life gains credence because of what it refuses to deny about death.

The Christian gospel is, first and last, a gospel of life. Here is a mere sampling:

"In him was life . . ." (John 1:4)
"I am the bread of life . . ." (John 6:35)
"He who follows me will . . . have the light of life." (John 8:12)
"that . . . we too might walk in newness of life." (Romans 6:4)
"And you he made alive . . ." (Ephesians 2:1)
"Your life is hid with Christ in God . . ." (Colossians 3:3)
"He who has the Son has life . . ." (I John 5:12)

We had occasion to note earlier in this book that many of the words of the prayer of St. Francis bear a weighted and not necessarily singular meaning: peace, love, faith, hope, joy—each and all of these Kodachrome words are transparencies that can easily get out of focus. So too "life" and "death." Christians surely have no monopoly on these words. Thus once more it is important to discern in what sense, with what focus, we are using them.

Take for instance the statement in which John has Jesus say, "Whoever . . . believes in me shall never die" (John 11:26). On its face that is patently absurd. Even the most frantic literalist could not possibly imagine that Jesus was saying, "Whoever believes in me shall never suffer cardiac arrest." Stethoscopes, encephalograms, and 100 percent death rates have quite as much to do with the most convinced believer as with the most ardent atheist. The question, then, is, What did Jesus mean? To an attempted answer to that we now turn.

II

Our answer is complicated, badly, by the worn-thin imagery of heaven and hell. People find it easy to think in spatial terms. Thus these highly important but also highly symbolic words, heaven and hell, continue to be misrepresented as referring to supra-geographical locations. Sometimes these descriptions, or distortions, have been replete with architectural drawings (heaven having twenty-four thrones, a high wall, and twelve gates) and with temperature charts (hell as a bottomless pit of burning fire). It has been more than four hundred years since the great Polish astronomer, Nicolaus Copernicus, decisively dismantled our three-storied universe and displaced the earth from the center of that universe. Yet the old imagery hangs on, to haunt, to hinder, and to falsify.

Biblical scholars are generally agreed that Matthew's favored phrase, "kingdom of heaven" and John's favored phrase, "eternal life," are roughly equivalent. The insatiable hunger of the Christian to know what heaven or eternal life is like is nicely greeted by a single verse in John: "And this is eternal life, that they know thee the only true God, and Jesus Christ whom thou hast sent" (17:3). That is a good deal more satisfactory than later speculation about pearly gates. It makes quite clear that heaven is not a future destination but a present possession, that eternal life is a matter not of duration but of quality. Eternal life commences whenever that knowledge and acknowledgment of Christ does. It stretches beyond the grave, we profoundly believe, for it is not limited by flesh and blood. But it begins in the here and now. Notice quite carefully, for example, the tense of the verbs in this word from John: "he who hears my word and believes him who sent me, has [not will have] eternal life; he does not come into judgment, but has passed [not will someday pass] from death to life" (5:24).

By the same token the death involved here is a death with a difference. The Christian's death occurs not when his heart gives out but when he gives out his heart, in love and obedience, to the Lord of life. Paul penned a one-sentence biography of the Christian life when he cried, "I have been crucified with Christ; it is no longer I who live, but Christ who lives in me" (Galatians 2:20). We are given a new center of gravity in a double sense: both a new center toward which the weight of our lives is attracted and a new cause for seriousness (not sadness, but seriousness). Gerard Manley Hopkins has left us a profoundly beautiful line, which he clearly learned from Paul: "Let him easter in us, be a dayspring to the dimness of us.[1]

"I live; yet not I, but Christ liveth in me" (Galatians 2:20 KJV).

"I died a thousand deaths" we so easily say. That is what it takes to be a Christian, to "die daily" as Paul put it (I Corinthians 15:31, KJV). Resolves so well begun are so easily forgotten, rationalized, or tailored to fit the passing moment. The awful, wonderful thing about making a gift of oneself is that it has either to be repeated or it is repudiated. Notice I used the phrase, "gift of oneself." The life in Christ is first a surrender and then a living out of, and a living up to, what that surrender involves and requires. The life in Christ is a central surrender, followed by a lifetime of smaller ones.

The pattern for this death by which we live is Jesus himself. He possessed a strong sense of being God's instrument. He was possessed by a strong sense of belonging, to God and to the people God had given into his care. How perfectly he is this pattern may be perceived by thinking of the prayer of St. Francis as a portrait of Jesus himself. Though hated, injured, doubted, and cast into darkness, he responded with love, pardon, faith, and light. Though no doubt often yearning for consolation and understanding, his greater yearning was to bestow it. He stands at the center of

[1] John Pick, ed., *A Gerard Manley Hopkins Reader* (New York: Oxford University Press, 1953), p. 12.

our history because he is its sublimest vindication of the truth, "it is in dying that we are born to eternal life."

Somebody has said that the amazing thing about the New Testament is that it was written without a single "In Memoriam" line in it. I have a higher estimate of Tennyson than that, but it is true that the respective atmospheres of the two documents are sharply different. Tennyson wrote the poem, you will recall, after the death of his dear friend and his sister's fiance, Arthur Hallam. Luke and Paul and the others wrote the New Testament after the death of their dear friend, Jesus of Nazareth. But whereas the poem is somber with chastened hope, the New Testament is vibrant with unchastened joy. They were not mourning the tragic death of a fallen leader; they were celebrating the victorious life of a Living Lord. Tennyson wrote:

> I stretch lame hands of faith, and grope,
> And gather dust and chaff, and call
> To what I feel is Lord of all,
> And faintly trust the larger hope.

Paul couldn't have written that in his darkest moment of discouragement. There is nothing groping or faint or merely hopeful about what this poet laureate of the gospel penned for mankind. He had known doubt, despair, and sadness; but he had sown faith, hope, and joy. He shouted, "Thanks be to God, who gives us the victory through our Lord Jesus Christ" (I Corinthians 15:57).

Paul was excited, almost overwhelmed by excitement, but that was because he was dealing with the most overwhelmingly exciting life in history. Dorothy Sayers, the late British mystery novelist turned theologian, wrote an essay in which she reviewed the life and death of Jesus: the birth during the reign of a hostile ruler, the attempts to assassinate him after his first sermon in his home synagogue; his words—now coldly scornful, now warmly compassionate, always quietly wise; the last meal with his wavering friends; the march to the place of execution. All this, she seems to be saying, gave Paul reason to be excited, for she concludes:

> If this is dull, then what, in Heaven's name, is worthy to be called exciting? The people who hanged Jesus never, to do them justice, accused Him of being a bore—on the contrary, they thought Him too dynamic to be safe. It has been left for later generations to muffle up that shattering personality and surround Him with an atmosphere of tedium.[2]

There is nothing in the least dull about the life Francis had found in his Master and for which he bids us to pray. This prayer, which has sought our attention throughout this book, builds from a quiet beginning to a crescendoed climax; from the major notes of love to the somber beats of pardon; from the melody line of faith to the counterpoint of hope; from the darting har-

[2] *Creed or Chaos?* (New York: Harcourt, Brace and Company, 1949), p. 5.

monies of light to the hurried sounds of joy—all this, under the practiced hand of its master composer, bursts into the symphony of its final line. "It is in dying that we are born to eternal life." Our lives are intended to be instruments for the glad playing of that deathless song.

It is a simple song, for all its patterned beauty. You can begin with joy and get to light; you can commence with hope and get to faith; you can start with pardon and arrive at love. And if you arrive there, at love, you have arrived too at that indestructible and undying thing we call eternal life.

Some readers will recall the book *Burma Diary,* written in 1942 and describing the flight of a large group of civilians and soldiers from Burma, just ahead of the Japanese army: "Today," the author wrote,

> we had to move the evacuee patients out of one hospital building into another. It was a filthy job because so many of the patients had dysentery. . . . It rains every day and no one has the resolution to start the cleansing job since he could never get the things dry. Patients, soiled bedding, soiled clothing all join to send up a reeking stench like a burnt offering to some perverse devil.

Then this refugee professor from the University of Rangoon continues:

> Three of us stood surveying the preparations for moving; an American boy who had joined the British army before we got into the war, his British soldier comrade, and I.

> We saw that the patients had to be moved. . . . If the others were feeling what I felt, we were all dreading to get on any more intimate terms with the stench and handle it. The American turned to his British comrade and said, "I am very glad at this moment that I am an agnostic."

But then Professor Geren concludes:

> Since he did not believe in the love of Christ he could leave the handling of these dysentery victims to the sweepers. Since his friend did believe in it, he was not free to stand by and watch. Nor was I. Get down in it! Pick the patients up! St. Francis kissed the beggars' sores. However this ended in him, it must have begun as the practice of the only medicine he knew. There is no need to call this filthiness sweet, or to start enjoying it through a strange inversion. Only one thing is necessary: for love's sake it must be done.[8]

O Lord, make us instruments of thy peace.
Where there is hatred, let us sow love . . .
Where there is despair, hope . . .
For . . . it is in dying that we are born to
eternal life. Amen.

---

[8] Paul Geren, *Burma Diary* (New York: Harper, 1943), pp. 51-52.

Index